STEPPING INTO SCIENCE

MAGNETS

By Illa Podendorf

Illustrations by Jim Temple

CHILDRENS PRESS, CHICAGO

ESEA II - '74

Illa Podendorf, former Chairman of the Science Department of the Laboratory Schools, University of Chicago, has prepared this series of books with emphasis on the processes of science. The content is selected from the main branches of science—biology, physics, and chemistry—but the thrust is on the process skills which are essential in scientific work. Some of the processes emphasized are observing, classifying, communicating, measuring, inferring, and predicting. The treatment is intellectually stimulating which makes it occupy an active part in a child's thinking. This is important in all general education of children.

This book, MAGNETS, emphasizes observations which can be made through activities. Many characteristics of objects are not otherwise observable. Magnetism is one of them.

Library of Congress Catalog Card Number: 72-148587

5 6 7 8 9 10 11 12 13 14 15 16 17 18 19 20 21 22 23 24 25 R 75 74

CONTENTS

Know a Magnet When
You See One? 5

Magnets Will Attract Some Things,
and not Others 11

One Way to Measure a
Magnet's Pull 18

Know What Magnets Will
Pull Through? 24

Know About the Poles
of Magnets? 29

Magnets Are Useful 42

Some Things to Do 46

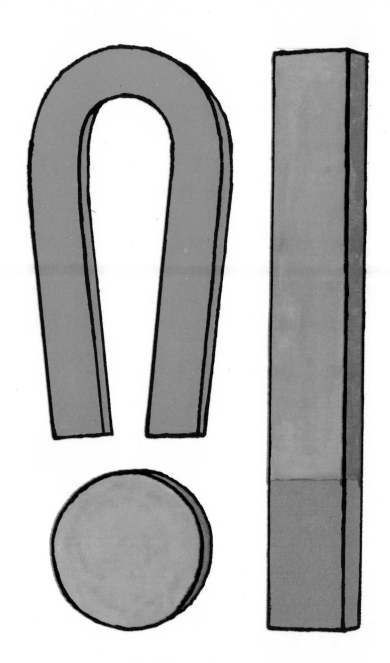

KNOW A MAGNET

WHEN YOU SEE ONE?

Look at these pictures. Do you know what they are? Are any of them magnets? Are you sure?

Here are pictures of two more
things. Do you know what they are?
Could they be magnets? Or are
they just stones? Are you sure?
Do you know a way to find out
whether any of the things on pages
4 and 6 are magnets?

Could you tell by the color?
Could you tell by the shape?
Could you tell by the feel of them?
Or would you test them in some way?

Max tested each of them with a pin.
He held each of them over a pin.
Each of them attracted the pin.
He was sure that each of them was
a magnet. He was surprised because
two of them looked like stones.

There is a kind of stone that comes from within the earth that attracts things just as magnets do.

It is called *lodestone*.

Now do you know a name for all the things on pages 4 and 6?

Could you call all of them magnets? All of them attract the pin.

All the things on pages 4 and 6 are magnetic. But you cannot know this without testing them.

MAGNETS WILL ATTRACT SOME THINGS
AND NOT OTHERS

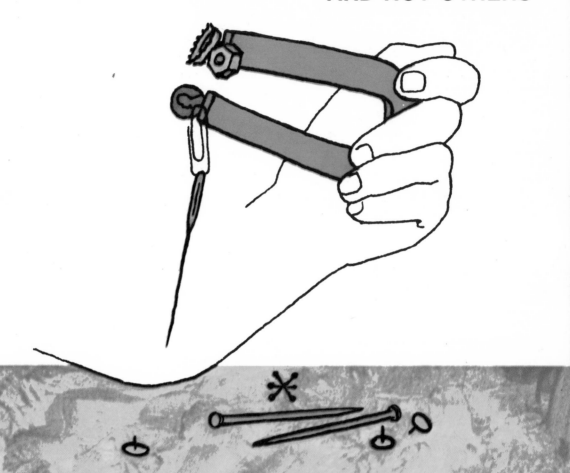

The pin had iron or steel in it.
All the things on this page have
iron or steel in them. Does this
give you an idea about what magnets
will pick up?

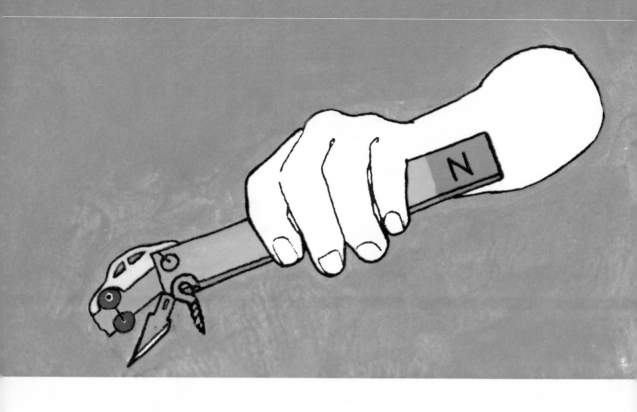

Here are more things with iron
or steel in them.

Now what do you think?

Was your idea a good one?

Magnets do pick up things made
of iron or steel. This is a good
thing to remember.

What about these things? They
are not made of iron or steel.
Max tries, but his magnet will not
pick up any of them.

Max had some pins and some pennies.
He said, "My magnet will pick up
the pins. They are iron or steel. It
will not pick up the pennies. They are
made of copper."

What happened?

Not all pins are made of iron
or steel, and not all pennies are
made of the same thing. Max had
a few old ones that his magnet
would attract.

If you have a magnet of your own,
test the things in your room at
home or at school. How many of
them have iron or steel in them?

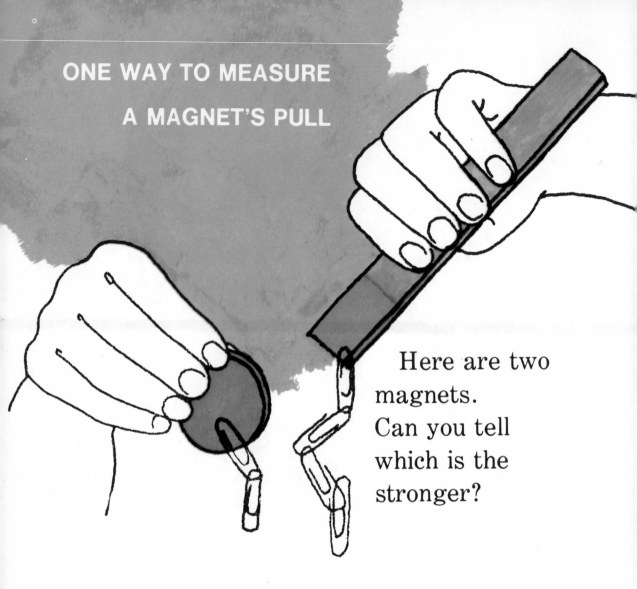

ONE WAY TO MEASURE A MAGNET'S PULL

Here are two magnets. Can you tell which is the stronger?

If you count the paper clips, it is easy to see that the larger one holds more of them.

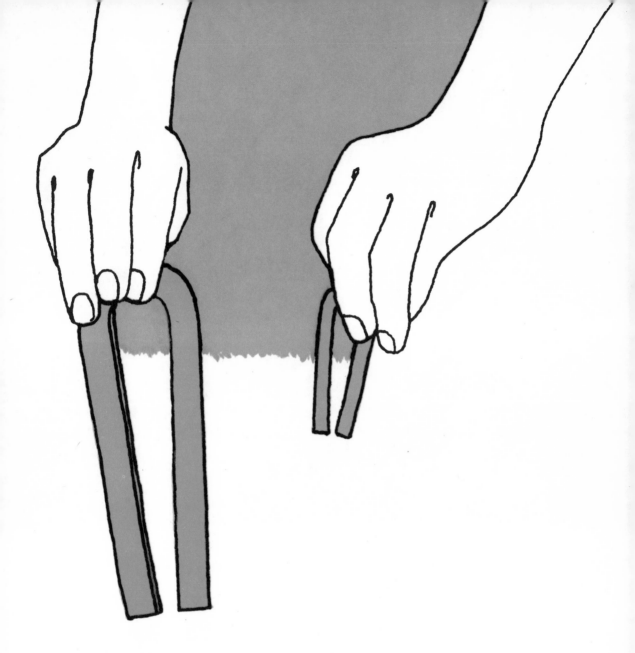

Here are two more magnets. Now
can you tell which is stronger?

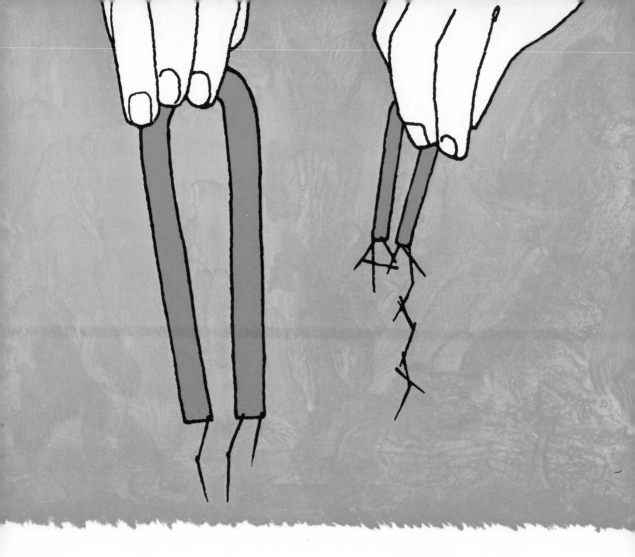

Count the pins. It is easy to
see that the smaller of the two
magnets holds more pins. We cannot
tell by looking at a magnet how
many pins it will hold at once.
We only can tell by testing it.

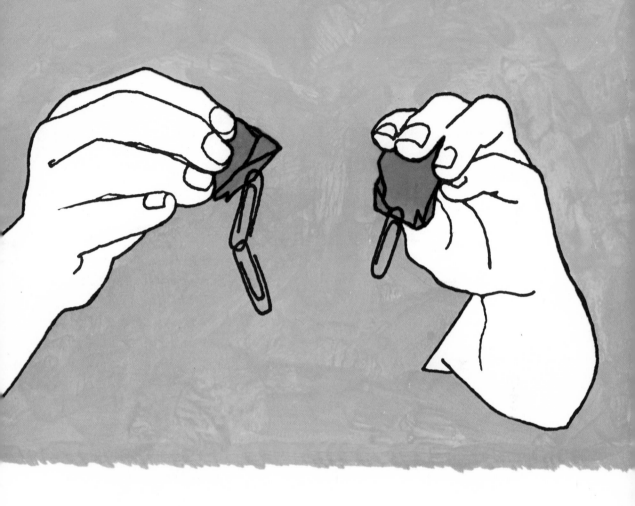

Here are two pieces of lodestone.
Can you tell from the picture which
is the stronger?

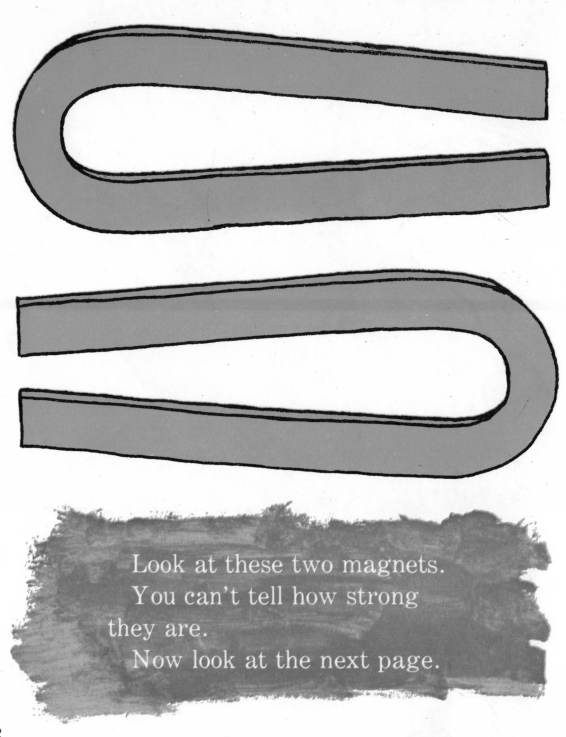

Look at these two magnets.
You can't tell how strong
they are.
Now look at the next page.

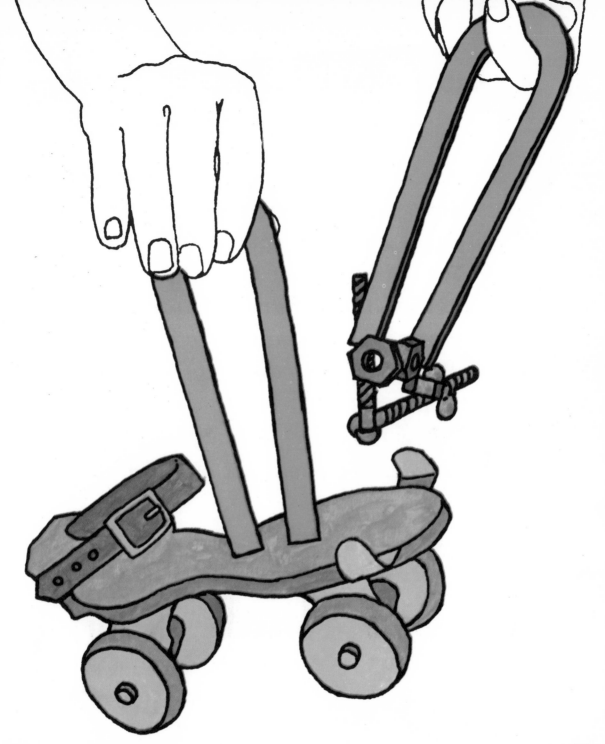

KNOW WHAT MAGNETS

WILL PULL THROUGH?

Suppose that you dropped your little magnet in a bottle of water.

You did not want to spill the water, and your hand was too big to reach into the bottle.

What could you do to rescue your magnet?

You could do what Max did.

He pulled his magnet out with another magnet.

Can you think of another way?

Could a piece of iron or steel be used?

Now you know that magnets will pull through water.

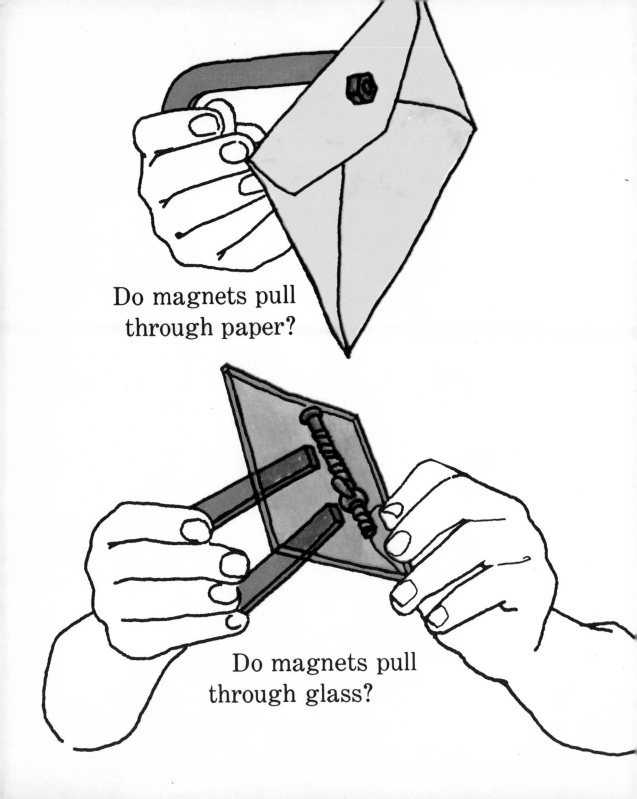

Do magnets pull
through paper?

Do magnets pull
through glass?

See whether
your magnet will
pull through cloth
and other things.

What kind of a toy car will your magnet pull out of sand?

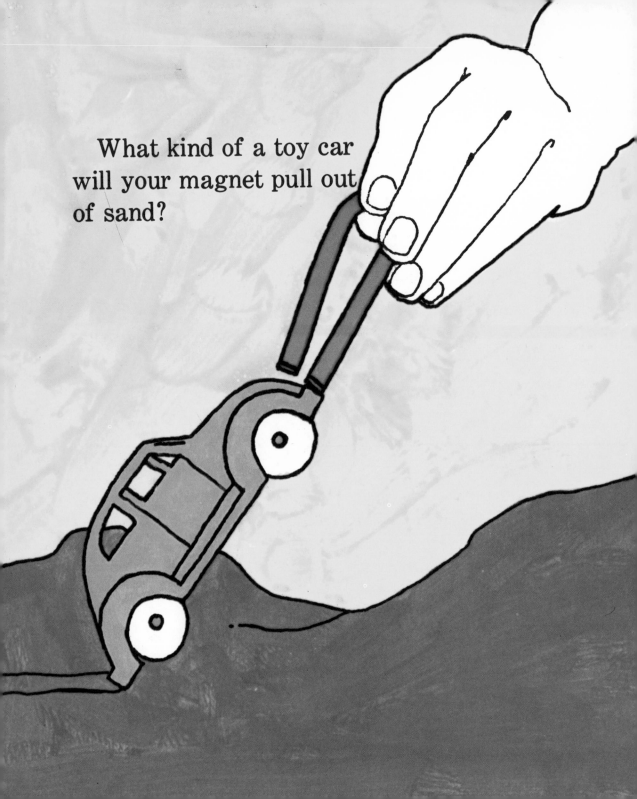

KNOW ABOUT THE POLES OF MAGNETS?

Look carefully at this bar magnet.
You will see a letter N on one end,
and the letter S on the other.

These letters are the names for the
ends of the magnet, or its *poles*.

Perhaps you wonder why they are called N and S poles.

The picture on the next page will give you an idea of the answer.

When a magnet hangs so that it swings freely, and there is no iron or steel near it, it will stay in one position.

One end will point to the North.

One end will point to the South.

The end that points north is called the north-seeking pole, or the N pole.

The one that points south is called the south-seeking pole or the S pole.

This picture tells you something more about the poles of a magnet.

Can you see that the N pole of one magnet is pushing away from the N pole of another magnet?

Two S poles will push away from each other, too. This is called *repelling*.

An N pole and an S pole attract each other.

These toys are made to move
because poles which are alike
repel each other, and poles that
are not alike attract each other.

You are almost sure to think
that some of the pictures on these
pages are of things that are magnetic.

Would you believe that they all are
pictures of magnets?

If you could test them you would
find that this is true.

Some of them have unusual shapes,
but they all have N and S poles.

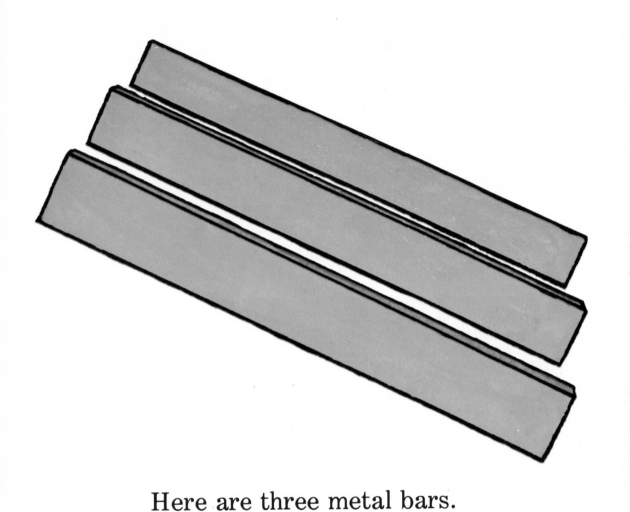

Here are three metal bars.
Perhaps you think they look like
magnets. If you had three such
bars, what could you do to find out
whether they have magnetism?

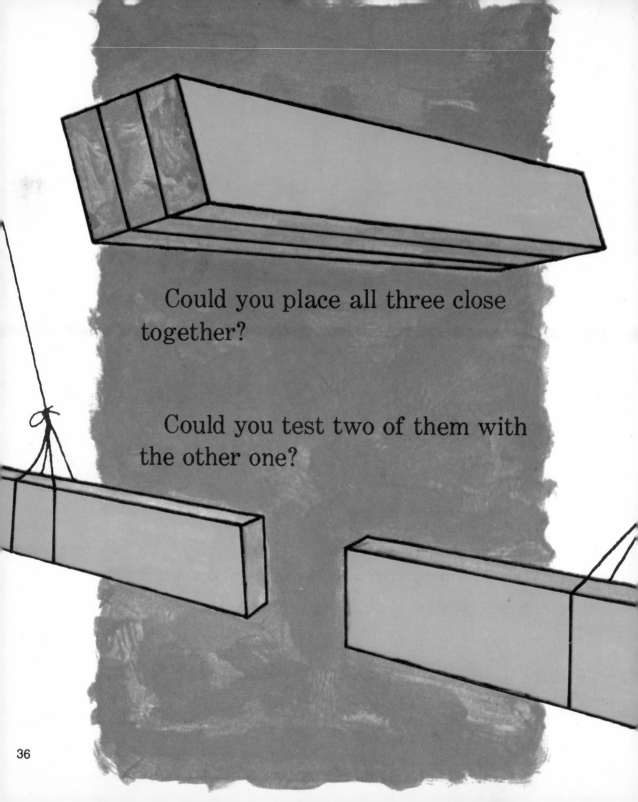

Could you place all three close together?

Could you test two of them with the other one?

Could you test each of them with
a steel pin?

Did you notice that
two of them picked up the pin,
but that the other one did not?

This means that only two of them
were magnets.

When you held all three together,
you may have thought that they all
were magnets.

When you tested two of them
with the other one, you may have
thought that they were all magnets.

You may think it is hard to test
for magnetism unless you have a pin,
or something else made of iron or steel.

Could you tell which bars were magnets if you had nothing of iron or steel to use to test them?

There is a way. Remember that two N poles repel each other, and that two S poles repel each other.

If one bar repels the other, they are both magnets.

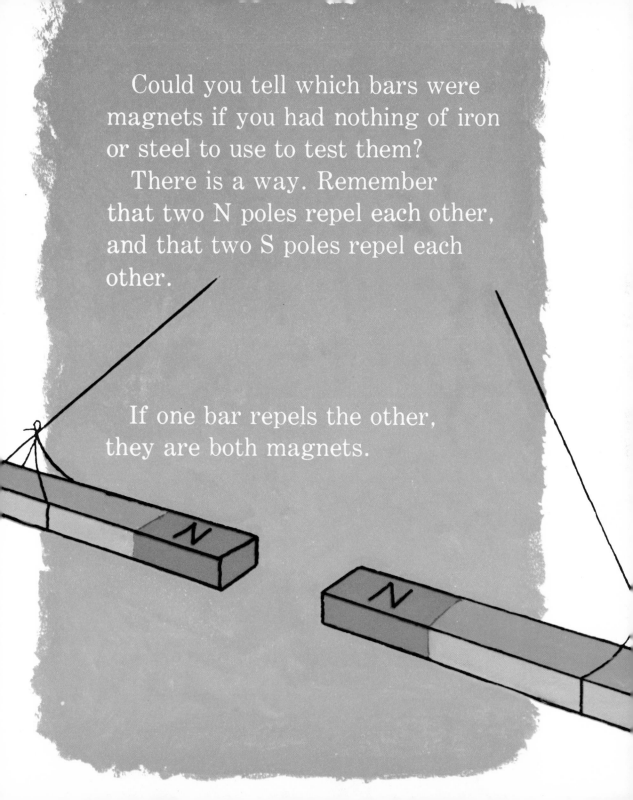

If you have a long steel needle
and a strong magnet, you can make
the needle into a magnet.

Stroke the needle with the magnet
at least fifty times. Use the same
end of the magnet each time. Stroke
from the same end of the needle
each time.

It is important, too, that the
needle is made of steel. Steel
will hold the magnetism better
than iron or other metals.

Does your needle magnet have poles?
You cannot tell by looking at it.

MAGNETS ARE USEFUL

Can you do these things with
your needle magnet? Can you pull
a pin from a crack?

This is a compass. Can you find a magnet in it?

Can you make a compass out of your magnetic needle?

It might look like this.

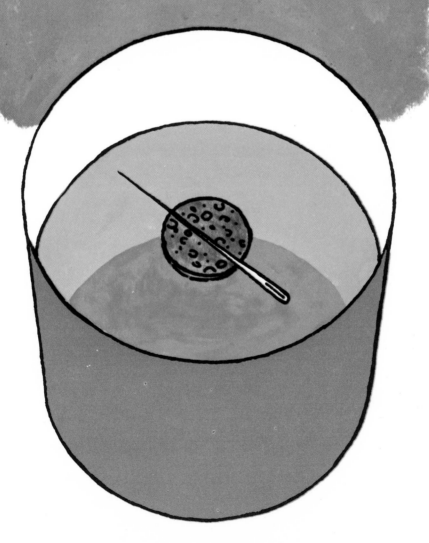

Look about in your home. Can
you find magnets in things like
those in the pictures on this page?

It is easy to see the shape of
an object. But you must test it
to find out whether it is a magnet,
and if it is, how strong it is, and
which end is the N pole.

All the magnets you have been
reading about in this book are
permanent magnets. That means they
are magnets all the time. Since they
are made of steel, they will keep
their magnetism unless something
happens to them. If they are dropped
or heated they may lose their magnetism.

Magnets should be cared for properly.

The picture shows how keepers should
be placed on them when they are put
away.

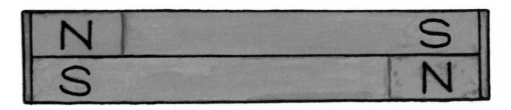

SOME THINGS TO DO

Collect as many magnets as you can find.

Arrange your magnets in order of size.

Arrange your magnets in order of strength.

Find a collection of materials and discover whether a magnet will pull through them.

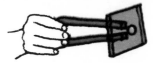

Make a magnet from a long steel needle. Page 40 tells you how to do it.

Put a magnetized needle through a piece of paper.
Hang it so that it swings freely.
Find the north-seeking and south-seeking poles.

Show that the poles of magnets
may attract or repel each other.

Show that magnets of any shape
have poles.

Make a compass by floating a
magnetized needle on water.

Make a floating toy with a magnet.